SUPER-SIZE
BUGS

WRITTEN BY
ANDREW DAVIES

PHOTOGRAPHY BY
IGOR SIWANOWICZ

STERLING

New York / London
www.sterlingpublishing.com

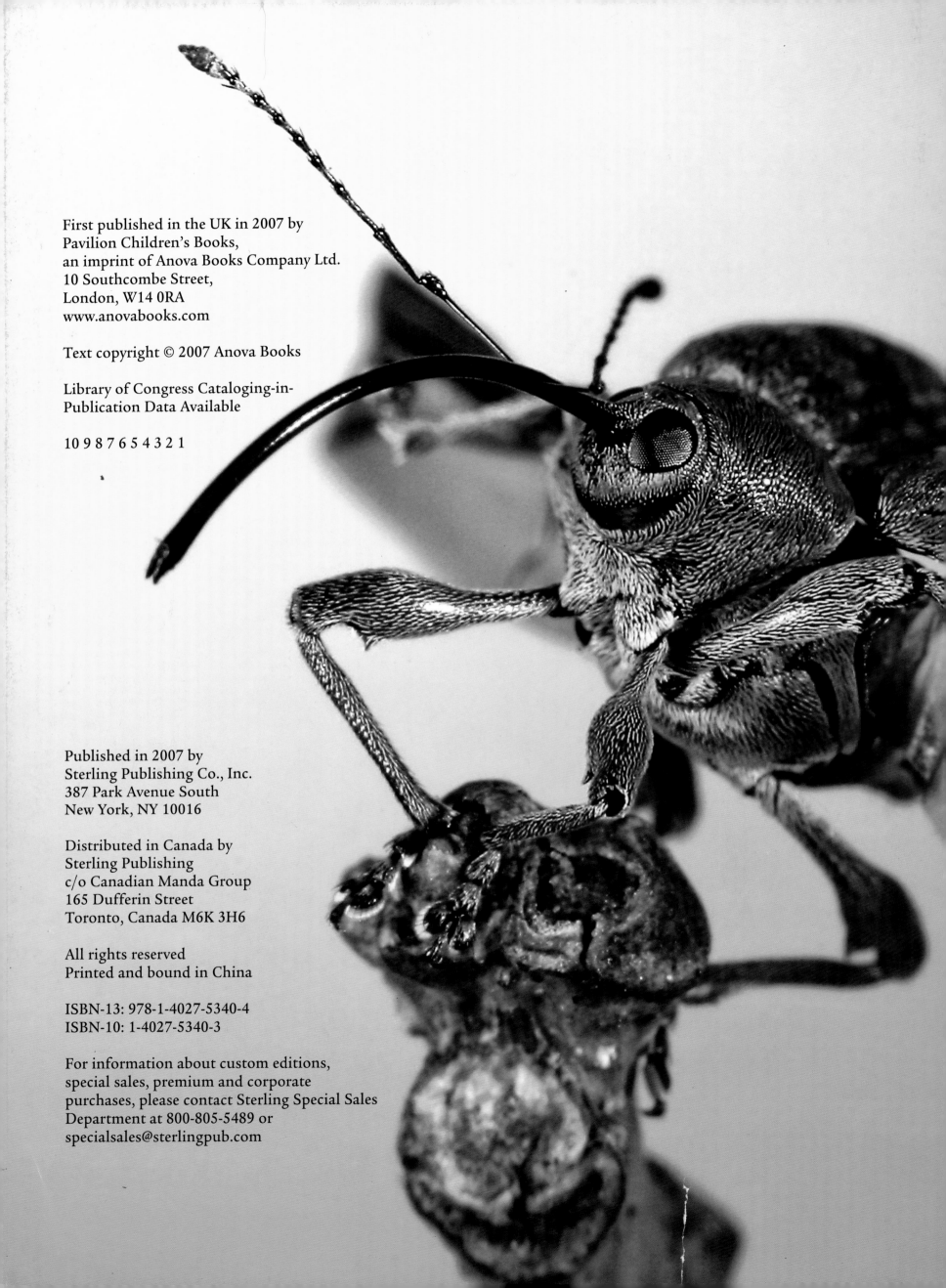

First published in the UK in 2007 by
Pavilion Children's Books,
an imprint of Anova Books Company Ltd.
10 Southcombe Street,
London, W14 0RA
www.anovabooks.com

Library of Congress Cataloging-in-
Publication Data Available

10 9 8 7 6 5 4 3 2 1

Published in 2007 by
Sterling Publishing Co., Inc.
387 Park Avenue South
New York, NY 10016

Distributed in Canada by
Sterling Publishing
c/o Canadian Manda Group
165 Dufferin Street
Toronto, Canada M6K 3H6

ISBN-13: 978-1-4027-5340-4
ISBN-10: 1-4027-5340-3

For information about custom editions,
special sales, premium and corporate
purchases, please contact Sterling Special Sales
Department at 800-805-5489 or
specialsales@sterlingpub.com

THE TEEMING WORLD OF BUGS

The world is full of bugs and insects. Counting centipedes and millipedes along with spiders and insects, there are over two million species in the world. And thanks to discoveries in the rainforests of Papua New Guinea, more species are being discovered each year.

Insects go to extremes!

Insects play an important part in the food chain. They eat up dead and living plants and insects and provide food for bigger animals such as reptiles, birds, and small mammals. They even form the diet of some aboriginal people. Because of their short life-cycle they can evolve quickly and adapt to new environments much quicker than other animals. They are found on the tops of mountains, in the middle of deserts, and some are even found in the Antarctic.

Unimaginable numbers

The largest order of insects is the beetle family with around half a million different species. It's impossible to be certain, but scientists estimate that ants and termites make up the biggest animal populations. Around 10% of the world's animal biomass (total weight of animal tissue) is ants, and another 10% is termites.

THE CATERPILLAR— AN EATING MACHINE

The insect's strategy for survival is to produce lots of eggs and hope that a few survive. Because they are near the bottom of the food chain only a small percentage will live long enough to mate again. From the moment they are laid as eggs, something will want to eat them for lunch.

A voracious appetite

While the larvae of ants, bees, and wasps develop in the relative safety of a nest, the larvae of moths and butterflies, also known by the Latin name *Lepidoptera*, have to survive in the big bad world. Moths and butterflies all start out as caterpillars, and often the caterpillar form looks nothing like the winged adult. Spectacular butterflies often come from very dull-looking caterpillars, and some fascinating

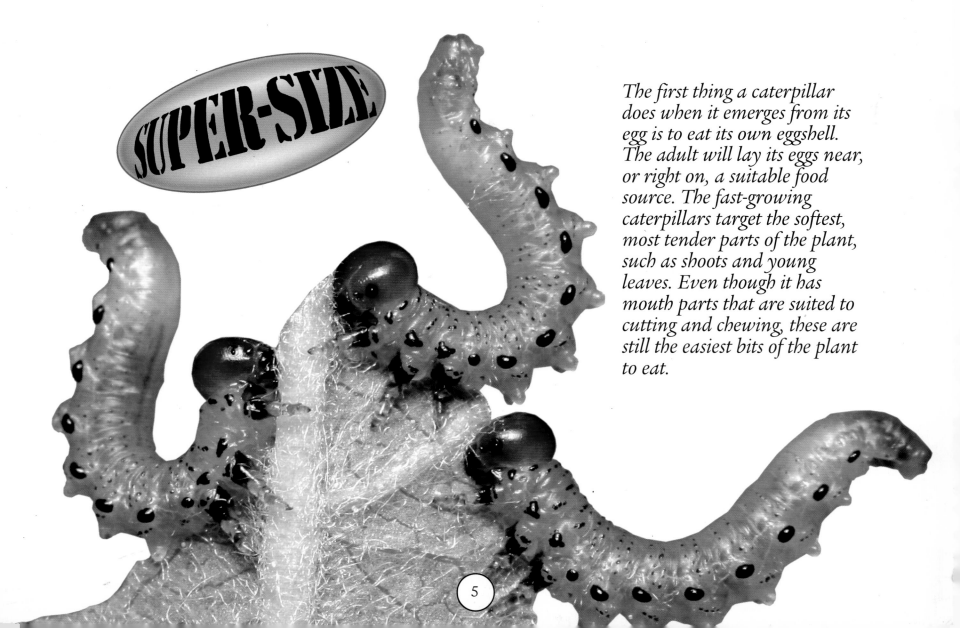

The first thing a caterpillar does when it emerges from its egg is to eat its own eggshell. The adult will lay its eggs near, or right on, a suitable food source. The fast-growing caterpillars target the softest, most tender parts of the plant, such as shoots and young leaves. Even though it has mouth parts that are suited to cutting and chewing, these are still the easiest bits of the plant to eat.

SUPER-SIZE

caterpillars, like the Woolly Bear, which is very hairy with two black ends and a bright brown middle, turn out to be very average-looking moths.

Caterpillars are like small eating machines and have to shed their skins four or five times before they pupate into their adult form. A Polyphemus Moth will increase its own weight by 86,000 times in two months. Caterpillars are also muscle-bound. While humans have around 630 muscles, caterpillars need 4,000 to control their multi-segmented body. A caterpillar needs an amazing 250 muscles in its head alone.

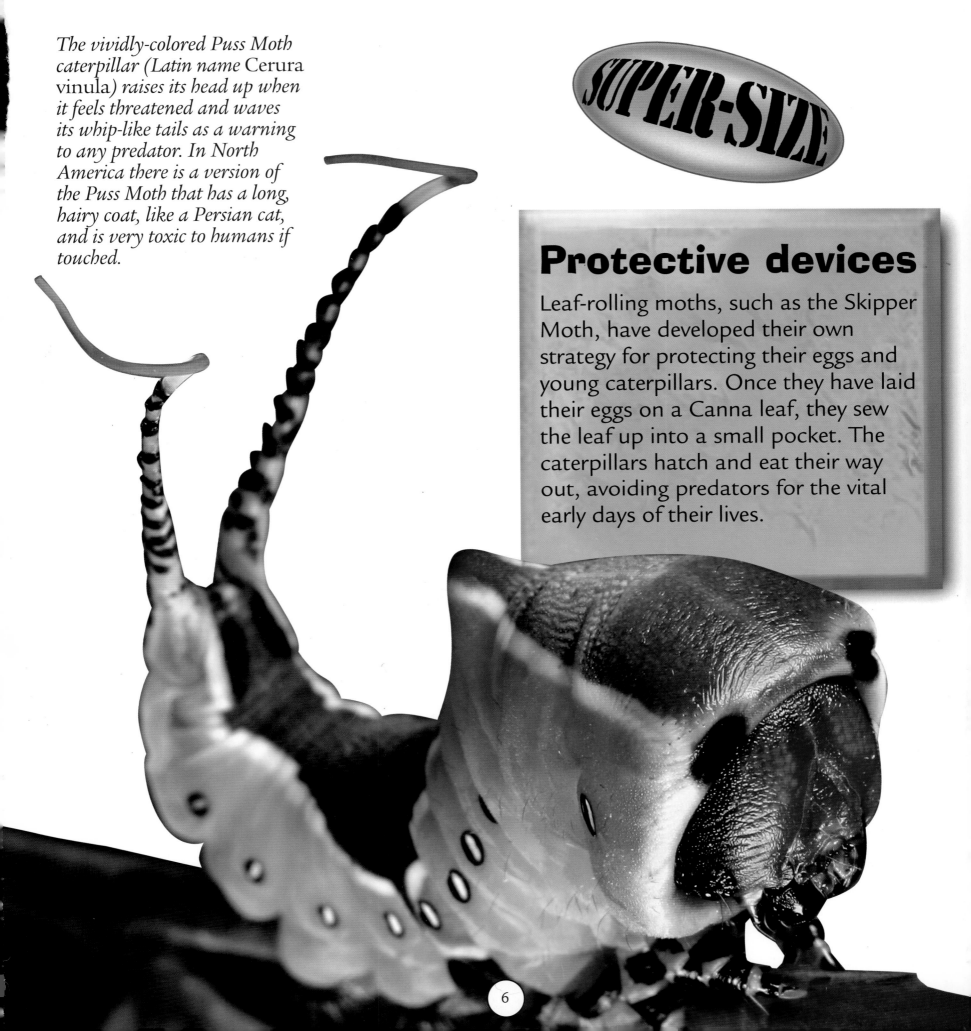

The vividly-colored Puss Moth caterpillar (Latin name Cerura vinula) *raises its head up when it feels threatened and waves its whip-like tails as a warning to any predator. In North America there is a version of the Puss Moth that has a long, hairy coat, like a Persian cat, and is very toxic to humans if touched.*

SUPER-SIZE

Protective devices

Leaf-rolling moths, such as the Skipper Moth, have developed their own strategy for protecting their eggs and young caterpillars. Once they have laid their eggs on a Canna leaf, they sew the leaf up into a small pocket. The caterpillars hatch and eat their way out, avoiding predators for the vital early days of their lives.

Contents

A Nut Weevil with its wing shields raised, about to take flight. The female uses her long snout to drill into hazelnuts then lays an egg in the hole. Once the eggs hatch, the larva feeds on the kernel of the nut until fall, when the nut falls to the ground. The larva then chews its way out and pupates in the ground over winter.

They're toxic!

There are many ways that caterpillars protect themselves. Some have eyespots that frighten their attackers, others use a silk escape line and drop from plants like spiders. There are caterpillars that look like bird droppings or twigs and blend into the background, but many more use chemicals for defense. Hairy caterpillars and brightly-colored caterpillars are often the most toxic because they are easily spotted and rely on their poison to keep them safe. Hairy caterpillars have spiny bristles or poisonous barbs that break off when touched. In areas of high caterpillar infestation the hairs can be blown off by strong winds and give skin rashes to passersby.

SUPER-SIZE

Like many moths, the lobster moth is named after the appearance of the caterpillar and not the moth itself. The lobster-like caterpillar is found on beech and oak trees in southern England.

Found in southern Arizona and Texas, the Calleta Silkmoth looks both beautiful and scary. After they pupate, the adult moths emerge at dusk and mate at dawn the next day.

8

SUPER-SIZE

This Tau Emperor Moth caterpillar is adorned with antler-like antennae, similar to the Hickory Horned Devils found in North America. Caterpillars can see very little through their primitive eyelets known as "ocelli." Most of the information they receive about the world around them comes from their antennae.

This picture shows the European Swallowtail Butterfly having just emerged from its chrysalis. In America it is known as the Old World Swallowtail to distinguish it from a number of other North American Swallowtails. In Europe, its closest relative is the Scarce Swallowtail, which is—not surprisingly—hard to find. The European Swallowtail is often found in the meadows of the Alps and in England.

SUPER-SIZE

The miracle of metamorphosis

Once a caterpillar or larva has reached its full size it will form a pupa and transform itself into its adult form, or the "imago." With honeybees, this metamorphosis is done in a hexagonal cell which the bees build and seal over with wax. Caterpillars anchor themselves in a sheltered place away from potential predators and disturbance, and transform their outer skin into a hard case known as a "chrysalis." From this case the adult butterfly or moth eventually emerges. The pictures above show the caterpillar of the European Swallowtail Butterfly anchoring itself on its host plant and then pupating.

The length of time spent pupating varies from species to species—the Monarch Butterfly pupates for only two weeks, while the Yucca Moth larva spend almost a year in its chrysalis. Many moths and butterflies in Europe and North America spend the cold winter periods in their chrysalis, only emerging when the weather warms up in the spring. As an experiment, scientists studying pupation prolonged the dormant period for the Yucca Moth and found that they could keep them in their chrysalis and still have them emerge after 30 years!

A SOCIETY OF INSECTS

One of the most difficult areas of insect life for scientists to unravel is the behavior of social insects and how they make their decisions. Though some bees can be solitary, the honeybee needs a large community to share the different jobs in summer. Wasps need large numbers to build their elaborate and beautiful paper nests.

Sharing the workload

A queen hornet has to start a colony from scratch each spring. She has to make the cells in her nest from chewed up tree bark, forage for food, lay the eggs, and feed the larvae until they spin silk caps over their cell openings. Once the first brood emerges, it takes over all the labor intensive duties from the queen and she can go on to expand the colony rapidly. Most hornets have a venomous

SUPER-SIZE

Busy bees

A worker honeybee will carry out a whole range of jobs in its lifetime. Its first task is to clean the cells so they are ready to take new eggs. After three or four days it will move on to the job of creating food for larvae. After six days it will take off on its first training flight. From six to fifteen days it will make wax and build honeycomb, and from eighteen days onward it will go out to collect nectar, pollen, and water.

sting and very sharp mandibles. They don't need to sting their insect prey, they just bite them in half!

Mutual Friends: The caterpillars of the Southern Purple Azure Butterfly feed on the leaves of mistletoe, hiding in the nests of Sugar Ants at the base of the host tree during the day and emerging at night to feed. Colonies of 50 or more larvae can live in a single ant nest. The photo below shows an ant tending a Purple Azure chrysalis. Certain species of treehoppers are also protected by ants. In return for protection, the treehoppers produce "honeydew," a kind of sugary sap that the ants consume.

This photo shows a cathedral-like termite mound measuring over 10 feet (3 meters) in height. Termites eat dead wood, plant material, and sometimes soil. The largest mounds can be up to 22 feet (6 meters) tall. Termites can be either workers who perform all the food collecting duties and storage activities, or soldiers who guard the colony against invasive ants. The jaws of the soldier termites are so big that they cannot feed themselves and have to rely on being fed by the workers. The main purpose of each termite mound design is to keep the young termite brood at a constant temperature.

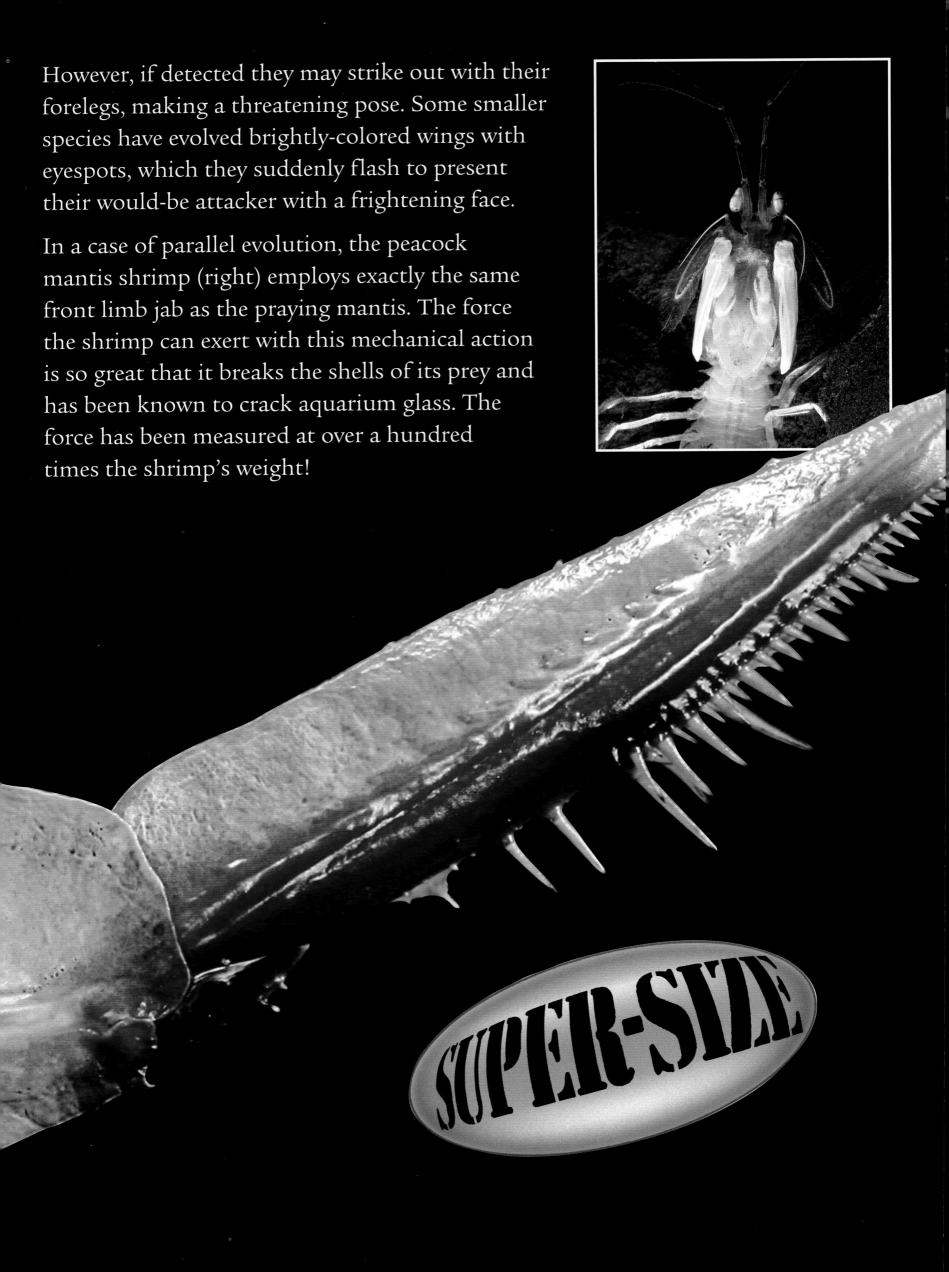

However, if detected they may strike out with their forelegs, making a threatening pose. Some smaller species have evolved brightly-colored wings with eyespots, which they suddenly flash to present their would-be attacker with a frightening face.

In a case of parallel evolution, the peacock mantis shrimp (right) employs exactly the same front limb jab as the praying mantis. The force the shrimp can exert with this mechanical action is so great that it breaks the shells of its prey and has been known to crack aquarium glass. The force has been measured at over a hundred times the shrimp's weight!

SUPER-SIZE

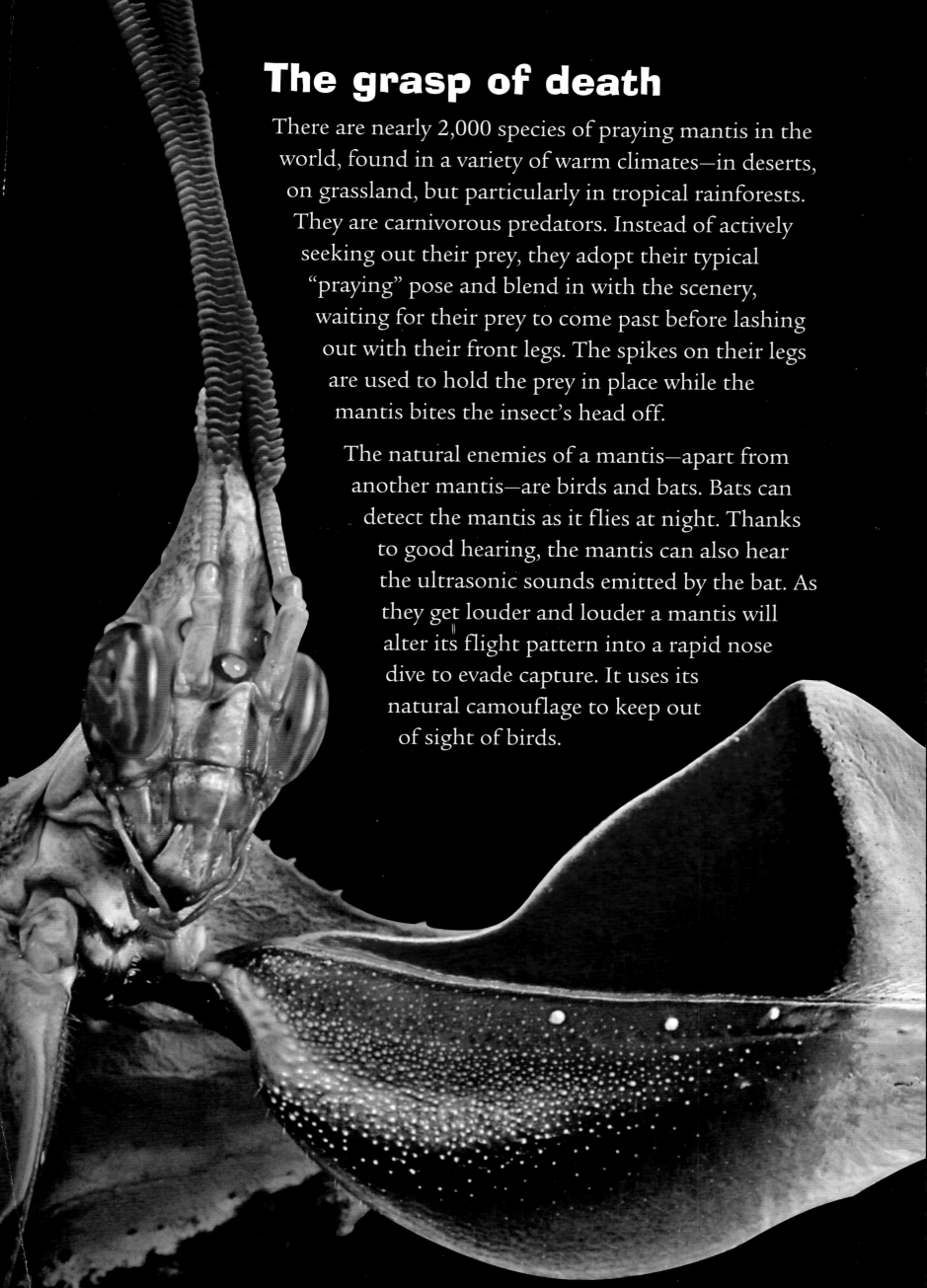

The grasp of death

There are nearly 2,000 species of praying mantis in the world, found in a variety of warm climates—in deserts, on grassland, but particularly in tropical rainforests. They are carnivorous predators. Instead of actively seeking out their prey, they adopt their typical "praying" pose and blend in with the scenery, waiting for their prey to come past before lashing out with their front legs. The spikes on their legs are used to hold the prey in place while the mantis bites the insect's head off.

The natural enemies of a mantis—apart from another mantis—are birds and bats. Bats can detect the mantis as it flies at night. Thanks to good hearing, the mantis can also hear the ultrasonic sounds emitted by the bat. As they get louder and louder a mantis will alter its flight pattern into a rapid nose dive to evade capture. It uses its natural camouflage to keep out of sight of birds.

KING OF PREDATORS

Praying mantises are carnivorous insects. They come in all shapes and sizes, some have spooky, alien-like heads while others look just plain goofy. Some resemble shriveled-up leaves, such as the Dead Leaf Mantis, while the Malaysian Orchid Mantis disguises itself as an orchid bloom, ready and waiting for an unsuspecting insect in search of nectar.

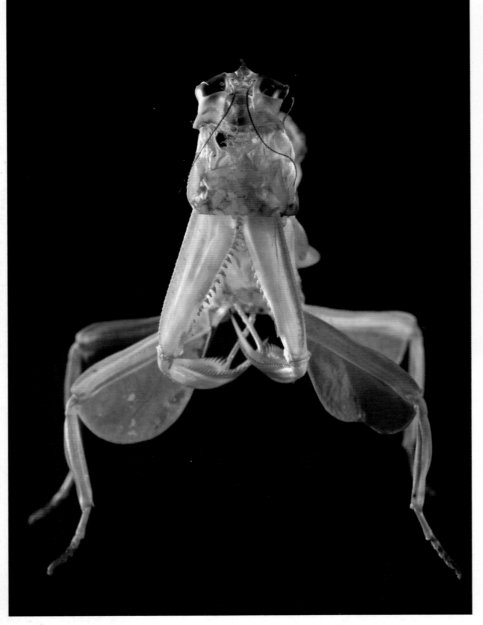

The young praying mantis emerges from the egg as a tiny replica of the adult. Like other insects they grow in stages or "instars," and when they reach the end of a growth stage and become too big for their skin or "exoskeleton," they have to molt. They push themselves out backward, leaving the old skin behind. This is usually done at night when they are least vulnerable to attack. Their new exoskeleton hardens in three to six hours. The photos show two views of a discarded mantis molt.

SUPER-SIZE

The larger mantises have slimmed down wings and rarely fly, but the Spiny Flowering Mantis often takes to the wing. It has eyespots on its wing cases to ward off potential predators and smaller forelimbs than most mantises. Its bright, adult coloration allows it to lurk near flowers and capture pollinating insects.

The picture to the right displays a Devil Mantis in a threatening pose. The alien-looking Devil's Flower Mantis (far right) is one of the largest and most sinister looking of mantises. It originates in Tanzania, East Africa and its Latin name is Idolomantis diabolica.

A Risky Business

The female praying mantis has been known to bite the head off her male partner after mating, so getting together can be a risky business for him. However, the mantis is a cannibalistic insect and *anything* that comes within range is fair game. In some species, the female stands guard over her eggs to prevent a parasitic wasp from laying its own eggs inside of them.

LIFE THROUGH A COMPOUND EYE

Insects' eyes are much different than mammals'. They have compound eyes made up of a number of different photo-receptor cells or "ommatidia." Each of these looks out at a very small area of sky, and the insect builds up a mosaic-like picture by combining the images they get from all of their ommatidia. Some insects, such as grasshoppers, only have a small number of ommatidia and have only a coarse, grainy picture of their world. Others, such as dragonflies and bees, have more ommatidia and can distinguish between objects quicker and from a greater distance.

A Bug's-eye view of the world

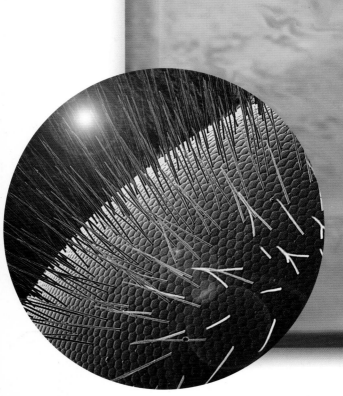

This shows a close-up of a honeybee's compound eye. Even though bees have relatively good eyesight their vision is still about 1/60th of the quality of the human eye. What we can identify from 60 feet (18 meters), a bee would need to be 1 foot (30 centimeters) away from. However, bees have a wider spectrum of vision and can see colors, such as ultra-violet, that we can't. That is why they are good at detecting certain flowers from which they gather nectar—their ultra-violet view of the flowers makes them easier to distinguish than if they had our normal color vision.

Who are *you* calling bug eyes...?

While the human eye has just one lens, an insect eye has thousands of tiny lenses, each one providing a small bit of visual information to form a "tessellated" or mosaic view of the world. And because insect compound eyes are on hemispheres with ommatidia pointing in all directions, they have a much better field of vision. While humans have a field of vision somewhere around 180 degrees, flies can see almost 360 degrees. This makes them particularly good at detecting the smallest amount of movement.

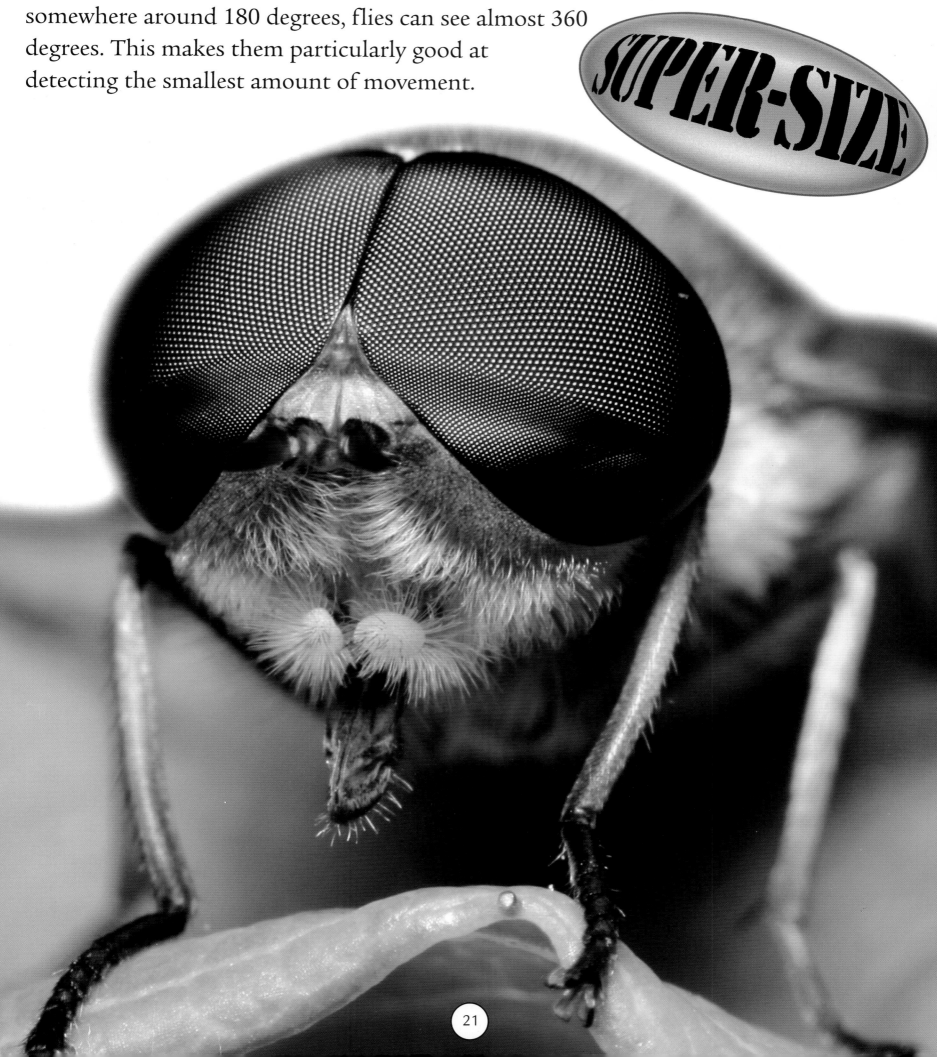

SUPER-SIZE

SPIDERS: LEAN, MEAN KILLING MACHINES

Spiders are different from insects in that they have two body segments and eight legs, while insects typically have three body segments and six legs. Spiders can all produce silk even if they don't use it to build webs. Their silk is used to line burrows, wrap up spider eggs, descend, or most vicious of all, wrap their paralyzed prey up tight!

Oh, what a tangled web they weave!

Spiderwebs come in all shapes and sizes. The most recognizable web is the traditional "Charlotte's web" spiral orb, but there are many more. Spiders will build funnel-shaped webs, sheet webs (like an orb web but horizontal, not upright), tangle webs, and single lines. The spider usually waits at the edge of the web because it doesn't want to be eaten by a bird, and waits for the vibration of an insect victim that has entangled itself in the sticky trap. Some spiders even build a hiding hole, with a leaf in the center of their webs. The American House and Cellar Spider builds a web that is so strong, it can support the weight of a mouse!

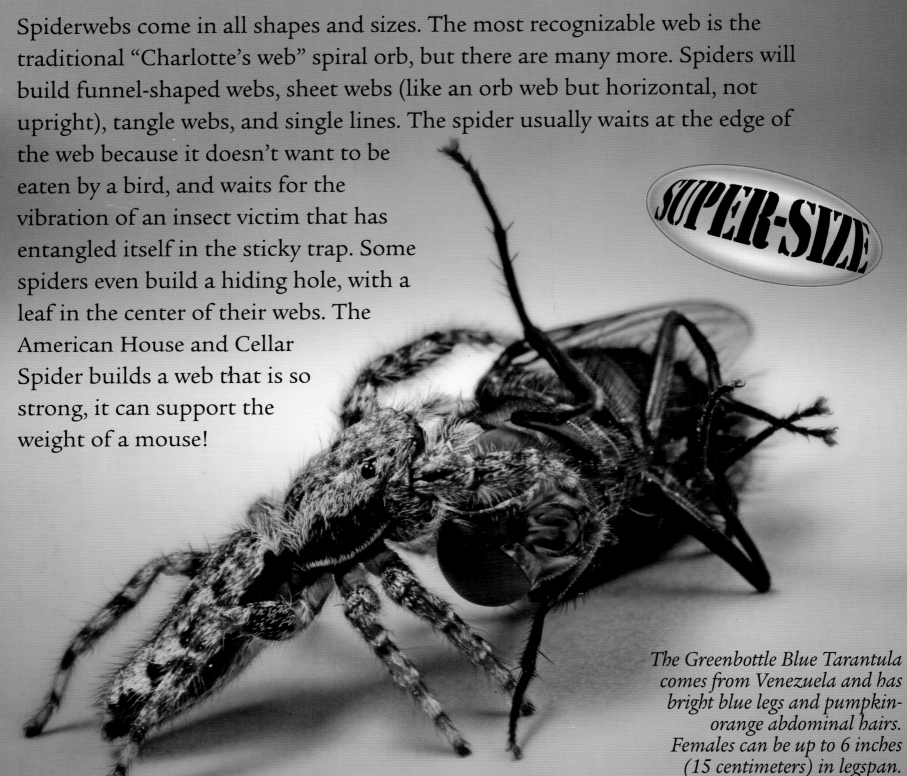

SUPER-SIZE

The Greenbottle Blue Tarantula comes from Venezuela and has bright blue legs and pumpkin-orange abdominal hairs. Females can be up to 6 inches (15 centimeters) in legspan.

This raft spider has the advantage of moss to walk on here, but on ponds and lakes where the water is calm, it can use surface tension to support its weight. Fishing spiders sit at the edge of the water with their feet on the surface, waiting to sense a ripple. When it thinks an insect has fallen in or a fish is surfacing, it rushes out to grab them.

SUPER-SIZE

A variety of entrapment

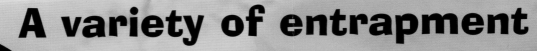

Spiders have a number of different techniques for catching their prey. Some build webs (Funnel Web Spider), others go out hunting (Huntsman Spider), some lie in wait ready to ambush prey that wanders past (Trapdoor Spider), and some combine web-making and hunting. The Net-Casting Spider (left) chases after its prey with a silk net that it weaves and attaches to its front feet and wraps around its victim before injecting it with poison. The fishing spiders and raft spiders are able to detect vibration passing through the water and can run onto the surface of ponds to catch small fish or insects that have fallen in.

The Brazilian Wandering Spider is equipped with the most powerful spider venom for paralyzing its prey. A tiny 0.00000021 ounce (0.006 milligram) is enough to kill a mouse. At over 6 inches (15 centimeters) in legspan it also looks like a threatening spider, unlike the smaller, but lethal, Australian Redback Spider. This exotic looking orb web spider from Sarawak, Malaysia has a non-fatal bite.

MASTERS OF ACROBATIC FLIGHT

Insects are the only animals without vertebrae that can fly. Given how fragile a butterfly wing is, it's amazing to think that the Monarch Butterfly migrates up to 3,000 miles across North America, traveling 50 miles a day.

Getting attention

An insect wing is an extension of its outer skin, or exoskeleton. Typical insects, such as a dragonfly, have two sets of wings called forewings and hindwings. In some species of insect, the wings are only carried by the female or the male. In others, the second set of wings has been adapted to

Halteres: a flight gyroscope

This Crane Fly shows an aspect of all insect wings—they are always attached to the second and third segment of the insect's thorax. The Crane Fly uses its second tiny set of wings or "halteres" to balance itself during flight. The halteres vibrate all the time and when the fly turns, it senses the pull of gravity on them. This allows it to perform aerial acrobatics. In aircraft terms it is the same as the instrument which shows a pilot at what angle the aircraft is pointing in relation to the horizon.

help flight (see the Crane Fly, below left). With many beetles, the forewings have been adapted to form wing sheaths (see the beetle below). These sheaths keep them protected when they're not in use. Some insects even use their spread out wings to warm themselves up.

The veins in an insect wing are there to strengthen them and also to carry insect blood or "hemolymph" to the thin tissue of the wing. The shape, color, size, and pattern of veins are useful for scientists to distinguish between different species.

SUPER-SIZE

CAMOUFLAGE AND PROTECTION

Bugs and insects survive through a number of different strategies—some have tough, protective segments, others have tricks, such as startling eyespots, while a lot try to mimic plants and blend into the background.

Survivability equals invisibility

This Buffalo Treehopper gets its name from its humpback that makes it look like a tiny green buffalo or bison. More importantly, it makes it look like a leaf bud or a small leaf. On the right is a thorn bug. Sitting right on a stem, the insect looks just like a jagged thorn. Though the term "bugs" is used  to cover a multitude of six-, eight- or more-legged creatures, a true bug is one that sucks the juices from plants. So thorn bugs will spend most of their time on plant stems sucking away.

The Armadillo-like Amardillus bug, otherwise known as a Pill bug or a Roly-poly, rolls itself up into a tight ball when it detects a threat, leaving its tough armor plating to resist attack. When all is clear, it unrolls again.

This Snout-Nosed Katydid from Australia has one of the typical defenses of the species. Their cone-shaped heads make them a very difficult meal to swallow.

SUPER-SIZE

The difference between a moth and a butterfly is that a moth usually rests with its wings out flat, while a butterfly rests with its wings folded up. It's an important distinction because the pattern displayed on the wings is designed to protect them, either by camouflage or by mimicking a larger animal. The North American Io moth has striking eyespots that make it look like it has the eyes of a large predator to keep its own predators at bay. And while many butterflies have bright coloration on their wings that attract birds, the second they fold them up, they can merge into the background.

Look into my eyes...

Though they appear quite vulnerable, caterpillars have a range of different techniques to scare off a range of predators. Like butterflies and moths, some caterpillars have also developed eyespots, which with the swelling of the head can make them look like a snake. They are certainly not to be messed with!

Phasmids and the art of concealment

Stick insects have evolved to such a degree that in their natural environment they are almost impossible to spot. They are known as phasmids—the Latin name for phantom—because they can disappear so easily. Not all phasmids resemble sticks or twigs, though. Many look like leaves, flowers, or even moss. How they have evolved depends on their host plants, so in jungle forests where leaves are big, they can be huge. The Malaysian Jungle Nymph can grow to a massive 9 inches (24 centimeters) long and is one of the heaviest of all insects. Equally impressive is the Giant Leaf Insect (left) which grows to 3 inches (7 centimeters) wide and 5 inches (13 centimeters) long and

resembles a leaf on legs. The female stick insects often reproduce without fertilization from a male, a process known as "parthogenesis." So males obviously have trouble spotting their fellow stick insects, too!

It's not just phasmids that have grown to mimic leaves. This katydid from Trinidad also takes advantage.

A relative of this Australian Giant Prickly Stick Insect, or Macleay's Specter, goes one stage further than imitating sticks and leaves—it disguises itself as moss. The Giant Prickly Stick Insect makes a more striking subject. Although in its native Australia it feeds on eucalyptus leaves, the Giant Prickly Stick Insect is a favorite of hobbyist collectors because it can be fed plain old leaves.

SUPER-SIZE

LOCUSTS AND GRASSHOPPERS

There are many grasshopper-like insects throughout the world, so how do you tell the difference between them? The simplest explanation is that grasshoppers have shorter antennae than bush crickets and katydids, while locusts are a kind of grasshopper that change color when they go into swarms.

A plague of locusts

Locusts are feared in Africa because of their destructive ability. Locusts, like most grasshoppers, will eat all kinds of vegetation as well as other insects. The most feared locust of all is the Desert Locust, which has swarmed across areas of Africa and the Middle East since biblical times. The reason for its enormous trail of destruction is that it can fly quickly over great distances. There are two phases to its life. It lives a "solitary" life until it rains. The rain triggers the females to lay eggs and also causes plants to germinate and grow, a perfect food source for the newly-hatched locusts. If there are enough young locust nymphs feeding together they will bump legs, causing a series of changes in their growth patterns and behavior. This close "gregarious" contact of the young locusts, or "hoppers," makes them change color and form massive swarms which can

strip areas of vegetation, then move on. However, because they can only hop, they are not as destructive as the adults who can fly great distances to wreak havoc.

Doing the Legwork

Grasshoppers can jump for huge distances—up to twenty times their body length. For Giant Grasshoppers, like the one from Panama (above), that distance can be 10 feet (3 meters). It is the male grasshoppers who chirp in the evening. The short-horned grasshopper does it by rubbing a comb-like structure on the back of its leg against a ridge on its wing— a bit like running a stick quickly down some iron railings.

The name "Katydid" was given to the insect because the chirping noise it makes sounds like someone saying "Katy did, Katy didn't."

Beetles can "fly away home"

Beetles are classified under the animal order *Coleoptera* which means "sheathed wing." There is no better example of a sheathed wing than the ladybug. It looks like a standard crawling bug until suddenly it unsheathes its wings and flies away. To do this it must first raise its hardened forewings or "eleytra." These fold flat across the wings when the animal is not flying, protecting them and forming part of the tough exoskeleton.

SUPER-SIZE

The beautiful Blue Ground Beetle (Carabus intricatus) is a rare beetle found in ancient woodland across Europe. With deciduous woodland being replaced by coniferous trees, its habitat has been reduced over the last fifty years. Ground beetles find it difficult to spread and colonize new areas because they cannot fly.

It's the dung thing

Beetles are the waste disposal experts of the insect world. They can clear up animal waste, hunt other insects, and eat plants. The Dung Beetle is the most famous of the waste processors. Dung Beetles can be divided into three types depending on what they do with the dung. "Rollers" roll the animal dung they find into a ball and push it backward with powerful back legs. They use their dung ball as a food stash or to incubate eggs. "Tunnelers" bury their dung when they find it and "Dwellers," not surprisingly, live in it.

BEETLES: FORMIDABLE AND CHITIN CLAD

Beetles are the most diverse group of insects. There are more varieties of beetle than any other order in the animal kingdom. Some have lost their wings. Some, like the Diving Beetle, have learned to forage under water. Most are characterized by a tough exoskeleton, which is both flexible and hard to attack.

Tiger Beetles are ground beetles that have lost the ability to fly. They are found on shore margins and woodland paths where they can use their great speed, up to 5 mph. They are ferocious predatory beetles and they have the mandibles to prove it.

They're armor-plated

Beetles owe their success to their tough armor made out of chitin. This armor, or exoskeleton, consists of a number of plates, or "sclerites," which are carefully joined together. They allow the beetle, such as this female Stag Beetle (below), to move around without exposing a weak spot. The chitinous plates also have wax coatings which will make them waterproof, keeping water out, or in dry climates, keeping water in. Apart from shielding them from attack, it protects them from a hostile environment, too. Beetle fossils have been dated to 25 million years old and because chitin is not broken down by water, natural chemicals, or mammals' digestive juices, once their exoskeletons are made, they tend to stick around. Beetles also have some ingenious protection devices. Blister Beetles produce a toxic substance that makes them poisonous to predators while the Bombardier Beetle sprays an acidic gas from its abdomen if attacked. Large ground beetles, like the Stag Beetle, will use their pincers and go on the offense.

UNDER THE ELECTRON MICROSCOPE

Beyond the simple magnifying glass, the scanning electron microscope reveals a whole new world of bugs and insects that live very close to us. It can also reveal the structure of delicate insect parts.

Scanning electron microscope

The scanning electron microscope is different from a normal optical microscope because it gets its image from reflected electrons, not from reflected light. The result is a very detailed black and white picture with a wide area of focus. The pictures can either be viewed in their original black and white form or in color.

Sucker punch

This is a scanning electron microscope photo of a mosquito proboscis. The female mosquito uses its proboscis to puncture human skin and suck out the blood on which it feeds. It has two pairs of sharp, flexible cutters surrounding a pair of tubes; one is for sucking blood and the other for delivering a chemical that prevents clotting. Without this chemical aid, blood would soon clot and stop the mosquito from feeding, making it try a new spot to punch through.

SUPER-SIZE

The Great Diving Beetle is one of the most aggressive insects, and even its larvae are vicious predators. They eat insects, tadpoles, and even small fish. They live in small ponds and keep an oxygen supply trapped under their wings, visiting the surface every so often to collect more air by using the tip of their abdomen to collect it. They are able to fly and can move from pond to pond colonizing a wider area as they go. Occasionally they land on the shiny roofs of cars and greenhouses, mistaking the reflective surface for small ponds.

Goliathus orientalis

The Goliath Beetle: a record breaker

There may be longer insects, but nothing beats the Goliath Beetle for sheer bulk. They can reach over 4 inches (11 centimeters) in length and the noise of one flying past is said to sound like a small helicopter. The Goliath is a "scarab" beetle and comes from Africa, though it has a rival in size from South America. The Titan Beetle is a longhorn beetle and is found in the Amazon rainforest. It can reach 6 inches (15 centimeters) in length, or 8 inches if you include its antennae.

A prominent feature of scarab beetles is a triangular plate called the "scutellum" as seen on this Flower Beetle. It sits between the two wing shields and the front defensive plate or "pronotum."

It could be on your head right now, the human head louse (above) has strong front legs which it uses to grab onto human hairs. The female louse glues her eggs near the base of hair shafts. After 7-9 days they hatch out and the young nymphs start crawling around. At first they are transparent, however once they start feeding on human blood they gain a reddish brown color from the blood they have taken.

Discovering another world

This is a scanning electron microscope photo showing a mosquito egg raft with larvae hatching out. The mosquito lays its eggs one at a time and glues 100-400 egg cases together to form a raft that floats on stagnant water. A larva hatches from an opening at the tip of each egg case. The photo (right) shows the larvae as they have just emerged, pushing open the lids to their egg cases. They will live in the water, feeding on plankton, before developing into pupae, which are almost as active as the larvae.

THE SECRETIVE WORLD OF MOTHS

Moths and butterflies are closely related, but there are many more species of moths than butterflies. Generally speaking most moths fly by night and most butterflies fly during the day, with some exceptions. Moths are much more furry and hairy than butterflies. Most butterflies can rest with their wings held upright while only a few moths can, and most butterflies have club-like antennae while only a few moths do. Moths are often named after things they resemble. The Death's Head Hawkmoth (above) looks like it has a skull tattooed on its thorax.

Found in much of the eastern half of the United States, the Io Moth shows just how furry a moth can get. Coloration can vary from yellow to brown. The large fern-like antennae are highly sensitive scent detectors used to locate a mate.

SUPER-SIZE

Atlas Moths are cultivated for their silk, but the most common species of moth used for making silk is the Silkworm Moth. Farmers take the cocoon that the larva builds and spin the fibers into silk. They also use the Chinese Oak Silkmoth, the Assam Silkmoth, and the Japanese Silkmoth, which are all related to the Atlas. In Hong Kong, the Atlas Moth is known as the Snake's Head Moth, because the tip of the forewing looks like a snake's head.

Overleaf: The Robin Moth is the largest moth found in North America. Like the Atlas, it does all its eating as a larva, as the adult moth has no mouth and cannot feed. It lives for up to two weeks and its sole mission in this time is to find a mate and reproduce.

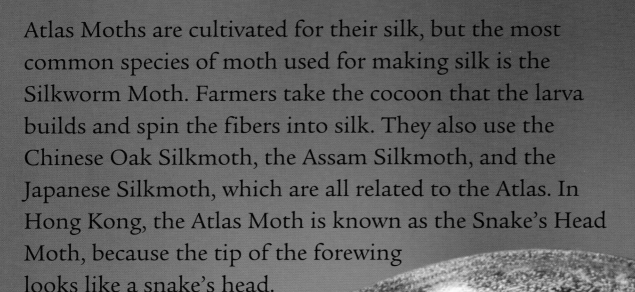

Smells like... another moth

Forget bloodhounds, moths have the most acute sense of smell. The male Emperor Moth can detect the pheromones released by a female at a distance of 6.8 miles (11 kilometers). The chemoreceptors on the male moth's antennae are so sensitive that they can register a single molecule of the female's scent.

The largest moth in the world

When it comes to wing size, the Atlas Moth is thought to be the largest moth in the world. Their wingspans are 10-12 inches (25-30 centimeters) in length. Its closest rival in size is the White Witch Moth. The Atlas is found in tropical and subtropical forests of Southeast Asia from China to India. When the female emerges from her pupa, she finds a place where her "pheromone," or reproductive scent, is best wafted on the breeze. Male Atlas Moths use their huge antennae to smell this scent and can detect her from miles away.

SUPER-SIZE

INDEX

Photography
The publishers would like to thank Igor Siwanowicz for his inspirational photography. Igor spent a weekend dredging his way through ponds just to get us the Diving Beetle photo on page 41. All photos courtesy of Igor and his Canon 20D, with the exception of: Oxford Scientific Films: pages 5 (top), 12 (top), 13, 16 (top), 24, 31 (top), 33 (top), 35 (top), 42, 43. Corbis: pages 10, 20 (bottom), 40 (top).